HARRIET
ROBINSON
SCOTT

FROM THE FRONTIER TO FREEDOM

BY DUCHESS HARRIS, JD, PHD

WITH SAMANTHA S. BELL

Core Library

An Imprint of Abdo Publishing
abdobooks.com

Cover image: Harriet Robinson Scott fought in court to
gain her freedom.

abdocorelibrary.com

Published by Abdo Publishing, a division of ABDO, PO Box 398166,
Minneapolis, Minnesota 55439. Copyright © 2020 by Abdo Consulting
Group, Inc. International copyrights reserved in all countries. No part of this
book may be reproduced in any form without written permission from the
publisher. Core Library™ is a trademark and logo of Abdo Publishing.

Printed in the United States of America, North Mankato, Minnesota
012019
092019

THIS BOOK CONTAINS
RECYCLED MATERIALS

Cover Photo: Chicago History Museum/Archive Photos/Getty Images
Interior Photos: Chicago History Museum/Archive Photos/Getty Images, 1; Jon Rehg/
Shutterstock Images, 5; Pete Hoffman/Shutterstock Images, 6–7; North Wind Picture Archives, 9,
22; Underwood Archives/UIG Universal Images Group/Newscom, 11; Red Line Editorial, 12, 31; Bill
Greenblatt/UPI/Newscom, 16–17, 43; Education Images/Universal Images Group/Getty Images, 20;
Sean Pavone/Shutterstock Images, 24–25; John H. Fitzgibbon/Frank Leslie's Illustrated Newspaper/
Library of Congress, 28; Tim Engle/Kansas City Star/MCT/Newscom, 32; Rob Carr/AP Images,
34–35; Everett Historical/Shutterstock Images, 38

Editor: Maddie Spalding
Series Designer: Claire Vanden Branden

Library of Congress Control Number: 2018964505

Publisher's Cataloging-in-Publication Data

Names: Harris, Duchess, author | Bell, Samantha S., author.
Title: Harriet Robinson Scott: from the frontier to freedom / by Duchess Harris and Samantha S.
  Bell
Other title: From the frontier to freedom
Description: Minneapolis, Minnesota : Abdo Publishing, 2020 | Series: Freedom's promise |
  Includes online resources and index.
Identifiers: ISBN 9781532118753 (lib. bdg.) | ISBN 9781532172939 (ebook)
Subjects: LCSH: Scott, Harriet, approximately 1820-1876--Juvenile literature. | Enslaved
  persons--Biography--Juvenile literature. | Scott, Dred, 189-1858--Juvenile
  literature. | Fugitive slaves--United States--Biography--Juvenile literature. |
  Slavery--Law and legislation--United States--History--Juvenile literature
Classification: DDC 973.7114 [B]--dc23

CONTENTS

A LETTER FROM DUCHESS

When I was growing up, I was never taught that enslaved people tried to escape. As the descendant of formerly enslaved people, I could not help but wonder if it was their fault that they were owned by others. I also wondered if they were satisfied with their conditions in slavery.

It wasn't until I was an adult that I learned that there were black people who dreamed of freedom. In college, I read *Incidents in the Life of a Slave Girl*. This book is an autobiography written by Harriet Jacobs. Jacobs hid in an attic for seven years to escape her slaveholder.

Fifteen years before Jacobs fled to the attic, another Harriet sued for her freedom. Harriet Robinson Scott and her husband had been enslaved their whole lives. They decided to fight for their freedom. They went through years of court trials before they were finally freed.

This book explores the difficulties enslaved people faced in fighting for their freedom. Please join me on a journey that tells the story of the promise of freedom.

Duchess Harris

A statue in Saint Louis, Missouri, honors Harriet Robinson Scott and her husband, Dred Scott.

CHAPTER
ONE

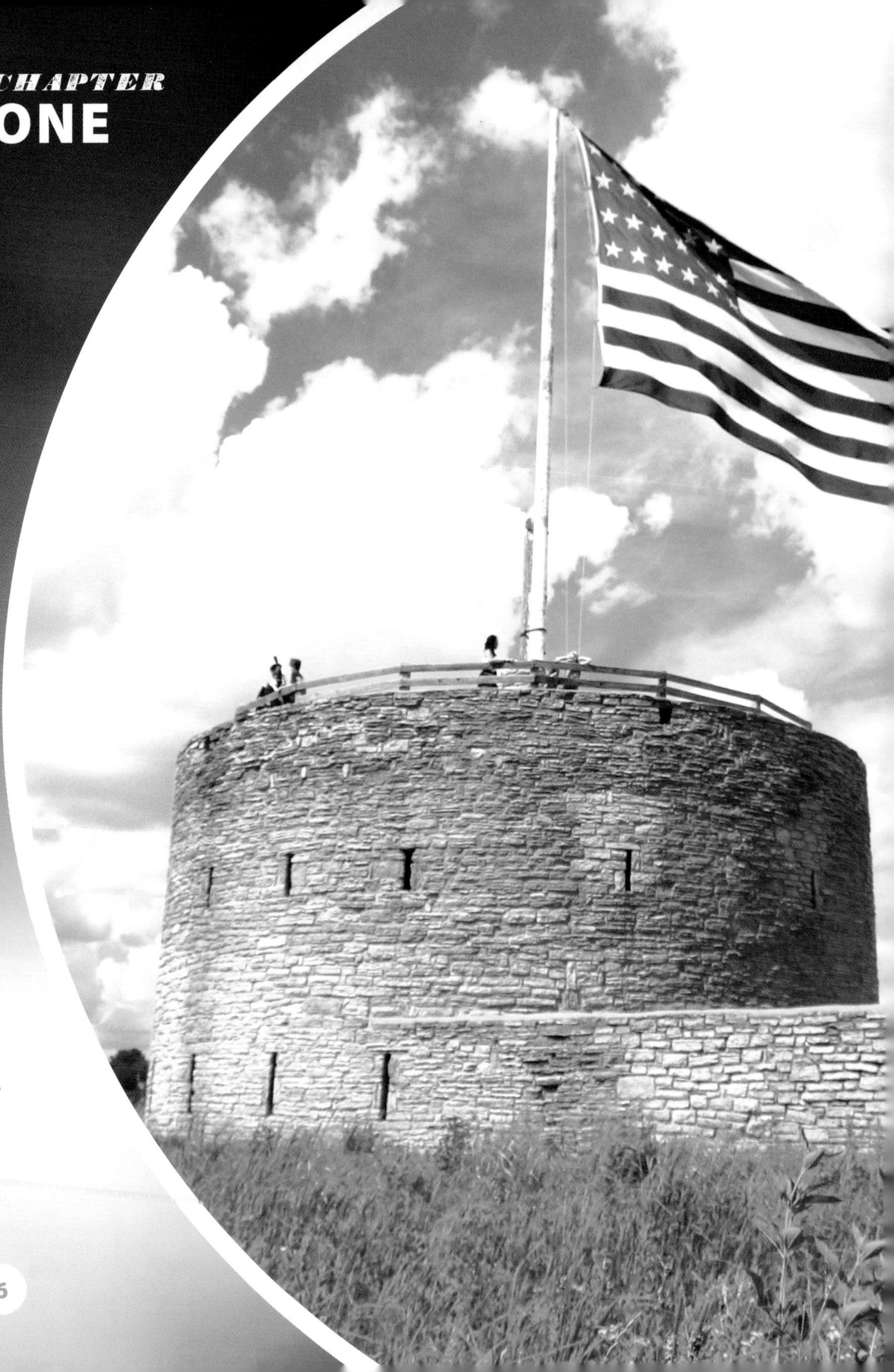

SLAVERY ON THE FRONTIER

t was 1835, and 14-year-old Harriet Robinson was traveling north along the Mississippi River by steamboat. Harriet was on the lower deck of the boat with five other black people. They were traveling with Lawrence Taliaferro, their slaveholder. Taliaferro was a federal Indian agent. He interacted with Native American tribes on behalf of the US government. It was his job to control the trade with tribes and keep the peace.

Taliaferro and his household were moving from Bedford, Pennsylvania, to Fort Snelling.

Harriet Robinson Scott lived for a time in Fort Snelling, located in present-day Saint Paul, Minnesota.

FEDERAL INDIAN AGENTS

The US federal government created Indian agencies in the early 1800s. The agencies controlled the trade between the United States and Native American tribes. Agents reported traders who broke trade laws. Agents were also responsible for settling disputes. Sometimes the disputes were between settlers and Native Americans. Other times, they were between different Native American tribes. But Indian agents often did not look out for the interests of Native Americans. Many agents tried to influence Native Americans. They encouraged Native Americans to give up their traditional religions and practice Christianity instead. Some agents sold tribal lands to ranchers and other nonnative people.

Fort Snelling was a military fort and fur-trading outpost located in present-day Minnesota. Native Americans traded furs with settlers at the fort. Taliaferro had been assigned to work at Fort Snelling in 1820. He traveled to the fort every year. This time, his wife, Elizabeth, was going with him. Harriet was going to work as her house servant. Because Harriet was enslaved, she had no choice about moving.

Native Americans traded fur with settlers in exchange for other goods.

Harriet had been enslaved her whole life. She was born in about 1820 on a plantation in Virginia. She had been sold to Taliaferro as a servant when she was a young girl. Taliaferro did not pay her for the work that she did.

Harriet's life at the fort turned out to be very different from her life in Pennsylvania. Taliaferro and his wife and servants lived in a house near the fort. Native Americans often came to see Taliaferro. Harriet had regular contact with members of the Dakota and Ojibwa tribes. She endured extremely cold winters. She did household chores. She dressed Elizabeth and brushed her hair.

THE EXPANSION OF SLAVERY

In the 1800s, the United States was expanding. Many people were moving west to settle new lands. Harriet was part of this movement. It began in 1803 when President Thomas Jefferson purchased the Louisiana Territory from the French. The new land stretched from the Mississippi River to the Rocky Mountains. It doubled the size of the United States.

Ojibwa Native Americans lived on the lands near the Great Lakes and and Great Plains.

For white Americans, this new land represented opportunities for a better life. Land in the West was cheap. Poor settlers could afford to own their own land. Farming offered them a chance to make a good living. For many people, the West symbolized freedom.

THE MISSOURI COMPROMISE

The below map shows the slave and free states in 1820. It also shows how the Missouri Compromise divided the land into slave and free territories. Areas south of the boundary line would have slavery. Areas north of the line would not. How does the map help you better understand the conflict over the expansion of slavery?

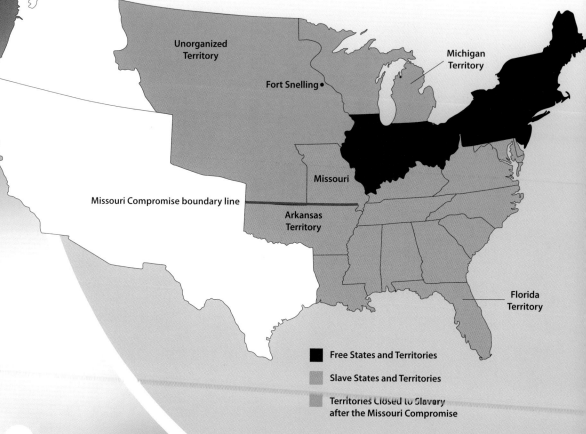

Unorganized Territory

Michigan Territory

Fort Snelling•

Missouri

Missouri Compromise boundary line

Arkansas Territory

Florida Territory

■ Free States and Territories

■ Slave States and Territories

■ Territories Closed to Slavery after the Missouri Compromise

But not everyone was free in the western territories. Some settlers took enslaved people with them. This caused a lot of conflict among the American people. Some Americans supported the spread of slavery. Others believed it should be outlawed in the territories. Some people believed slavery should be abolished altogether.

A COMPROMISE

The issue over the expansion of slavery came to a head when Missouri was ready to join the Union. At the time, the number of

PERSPECTIVES

A NEW UNION?

John Quincy Adams was the US secretary of state when the Missouri Compromise was passed. Adams was against slavery. But he supported the Missouri Compromise. He believed that Missouri and other states would leave the Union if Missouri was forced to give up slavery. He saw the Missouri Compromise as the only way to keep the Union together. He wrote, "I have favored this Missouri Compromise, believing it to be all that could be effected under the present Constitution, and from extreme unwillingness to put the Union at hazard."

states that outlawed slavery was equal to the number of states that allowed slavery. The free and slave states were represented equally in the US Congress. Missouri wanted to join the Union as a slave state. If it did, it would upset this balance of power.

A solution was finally reached with the Missouri Compromise of 1820. Missouri would join the Union as a slave state. Maine would join the Union as a free state. The Louisiana Territory would be divided. A boundary was created in the territory. Slavery was outlawed in most lands that were north of the boundary. Settlers to the south of the boundary could own slaves.

Fort Snelling was north of the boundary. But Harriet had been enslaved while she lived there. So had Dred Scott, the man she would marry. In 1846 Harriet and Dred would argue that living in a free territory made them free. They would use this argument to fight for their freedom.

STRAIGHT TO THE
SOURCE

Lea VanderVelde is a law professor at the University of Iowa. She wrote a book about Harriet Robinson Scott called *Mrs. Dred Scott: A Life on Slavery's Frontier*. In the book, VanderVelde explains why she chose to write about Harriet:

> Women's history is often necessary to complement the many histories that have been written about men. Dred's life story has been told effectively . . . but Harriet's life story was missed. . . .
>
> Harriet's frontier experience . . . is worthy of depiction because it runs so counter to the predominant slavery narrative. The tensions of enslavement on the frontier are set against a wilderness background of states coming into being rather than in a setting of cultivated fields, fences, boundaries, patrols, and established legal systems.
>
> Source: Lea VanderVelde. *Mrs. Dred Scott: A Life on Slavery's Frontier*. New York: Oxford University Press, 2009. Print. 4–5.

What's the Big Idea?

Take a close look at the passage. What reasons does the author give for focusing on Harriet's story? How is Harriet's story different from other slave narratives?

CHAPTER TWO

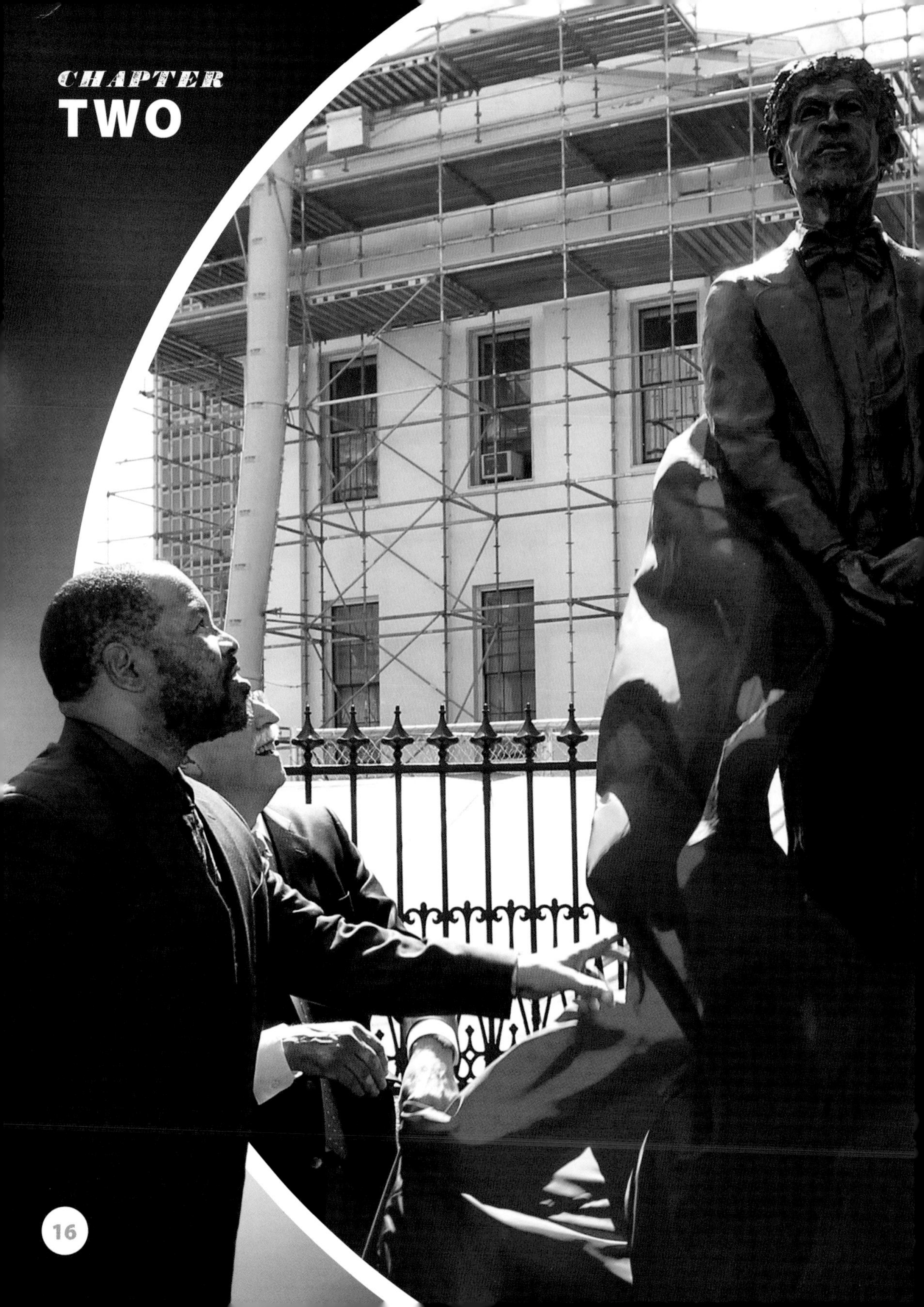

THE SCOTT FAMILY

I n the spring of 1836, Harriet met another enslaved person at Fort Snelling. His name was Dred Scott. John Emerson was Dred's slaveholder. Emerson was a military surgeon at Fort Snelling. Dred lived with Emerson at the fort's hospital. Dred was Emerson's personal servant. He prepared Emerson's meals and cleaned his living area. Dred also brushed Emerson's uniform and polished his boots.

Harriet and Dred decided to marry. Enslaved people were not allowed to have an official wedding ceremony. Instead, an enslaved couple could take part in a ceremony

In 2012 a statue of Harriet and Dred Scott was unveiled outside a courthouse in Saint Louis, Missouri.

in which they would jump over a broom. Then they considered themselves husband and wife.

Taliaferro was a justice of the peace. He could perform marriage ceremonies that were recognized by the law. Harriet wanted an official wedding. In about 1837, Taliaferro married Harriet and Dred. This made their marriage legal. Harriet was about 17 years old. Dred was about 40 years old. After the wedding, Taliaferro gave up his ownership of Harriet. Harriet moved from Taliaferro's house to the hospital at the fort where Dred lived.

Harriet's life had changed again. At the hospital, she did not encounter Native Americans. The hospital only treated soldiers. Each day, Harriet followed the same routine. She cooked and cleaned for the officers.

ON THE MOVE

Emerson did not like the cold winters at Fort Snelling. He requested to be transferred to another place where a surgeon was needed. In October 1837, he was transferred to Saint Louis, Missouri. He normally would have traveled there by steamship on the Mississippi River. But part of the river was frozen. Emerson had to go by canoe instead. He did not have the space to carry many things in his canoe. So he left most of his possessions behind. This included Harriet and Dred. He hired them out to work for other people at the fort until he could send for them. Harriet and Dred did

Visitors to Fort Snelling can see where Harriet and Dred Scott lived.

not receive payment for the work they did. Emerson received their pay.

Emerson was soon transferred from Missouri to Louisiana. In Louisiana, he met Irene Sanford. They were married in early 1838. Soon after the wedding, Dred and Harriet traveled to Louisiana to join them. Harriet was pregnant. She was expecting her first child.

The Scotts did not stay in Louisiana for long. A few months after they arrived, Emerson was sent back to Fort Snelling. The group traveled by steamboat up the Mississippi River. On the way, Harriet gave birth to a daughter she named Eliza. Eliza was born in the free territory north of the boundary established in the Missouri Compromise.

In 1840 Emerson had to leave again. This time he went to Florida. Irene and the Scotts moved to Saint Louis. They lived on Irene's father's farm.

Emerson returned to Saint Louis in 1842. Then he and Irene moved to Iowa. They left the Scotts behind in Saint Louis. Emerson hired out the Scotts to other people. Emerson collected their pay.

SAINT LOUIS

Saint Louis was much different than Fort Snelling. At the fort, everyone worked together to survive. Both the soldiers and the enslaved people had to take orders. But on plantations in the South, some white people did not work at all. They relied entirely on enslaved people to run their plantations. Many white people thought black people were inferior. Some African Americans in Saint Louis were free, but many were enslaved. The city was a major slave market. African Americans as young as seven years old were sold to the highest bidders.

Many enslaved people in the South did hard labor, such as harvesting crops.

In 1843 Emerson died. Irene became the Scotts' slaveholder. She continued to hire out the Scotts and collect their pay.

SEEKING FREEDOM

In about 1845, Harriet gave birth to another daughter. Lizzie Scott was born in Saint Louis. Eliza was now nearly eight years old. Harriet and Dred worried about their daughters. Dred was nearly 50 years old. But Harriet and the girls still had many years of hard work ahead of them. Irene might decide to sell the girls to another slaveholder.

Over the years, the Scotts had many opportunities to escape. Their slaveholder had allowed them to walk around Saint Louis on their own. Still, they had never tried to escape. But now Harriet and Dred wanted their children to be free.

In 1846 Dred tried to buy his family's freedom. But Irene refused to let them go. She could sell them or give them to her own children one day. She could continue to earn money by renting them out. Harriet and Dred decided to sue for their freedom in court.

EXPLORE ONLINE

Chapter Two discusses Harriet and Dred's lives as enslaved people living on the frontier. The article at the website below goes into more depth on this topic. As you know, every source is different. How is the information from the website the same as the information in Chapter Two? What new information did you learn from the website?

HARRIET ROBINSON SCOTT
abdocorelibrary.com/harriet-robinson-scott

CHAPTER
THREE

THE BATTLE IN THE COURTS

Harriet learned that other enslaved people had sued for their freedom and won. In April 1846, Harriet and Dred filed separate petitions in the Saint Louis Circuit Court. The petitions asked for permission to sue Irene Emerson for their freedom. Harriet and Dred believed they should be free because they had lived in territories where slavery was illegal. Similar cases had been brought to court before in Missouri. In those cases, the enslaved people had either worked or lived in a free state or territory. The enslaved people in all of these

Harriet and Dred Scotts' cases were tried at the Old Courthouse in Saint Louis, Missouri, in 1847 and 1850.

A FAITHFUL FRIEND

Henry Blow was the son of Dred's first slaveholder, Peter Blow. Henry and Dred were friends. In 1830 Peter moved his family and slaves to Saint Louis. Within a year, Peter's wife died. The next year, Peter sold Dred to John Emerson. Peter later died. Henry became an orphan at 15 years old. He worked hard and became a successful businessman. He also became an abolitionist. He did not forget his childhood friend. Years later, he encouraged Dred and Harriet to sue for their freedom. He also helped support them financially.

cases had been granted their freedom.

A judge accepted the Scotts' petitions. Lawyer Francis Murdoch took on their cases. He helped the Scotts get the legal process started. He also paid their legal fees. But Murdoch moved away and could not remain their lawyer. The children of Dred's first slaveholder, Peter Blow, stepped in. They helped the Scotts find a new lawyer. They gave the Scotts money to pay legal fees.

The Scotts' cases came to trial on June 30, 1847. The Scotts had to prove two things. They had to prove that they had lived in a free territory. They also had to prove that someone had deprived them of their freedom.

The Scotts' lawyer relied on the testimony of Samuel Russell. Samuel was a store owner. He testified that he had hired the Scotts from Emerson. But his wife, Adeline, was the one who had actually hired the Scotts. She had not been asked to testify, so there was no legal connection between Samuel and Emerson. Adeline's testimony could have helped prove that Emerson enslaved the Scotts. The jury did not think there was enough evidence to prove that the Scotts were enslaved. The Scotts' cases were dismissed. So their lawyer asked for a retrial.

A SECOND TRIAL

Harriet and Dred's cases did not come to trial again for two years. The Scotts were imprisoned for part

FRANK LESLIE'S ILLUSTRATED

NEWSPAPER

Entered according to Act of Congress, in the year 1857, by FRANK LESLIE, in the Clerk's Office of the District Court for the Southern District of New York. (Copyrighted June 22, 1857.)

No. 82.—VOL. IV.]   NEW YORK, SATURDAY, JUNE 27, 1857.   [PRICE 6 CENTS.

TO TOURISTS AND TRAVELLERS.

We shall be happy to receive personal narratives, of land or sea, including adventures and incidents, from every person who pleases to correspond with our paper.

We take this opportunity of returning our thanks to our numerous artistic correspondents throughout the country, for the many sketches we are constantly receiving from them of the news of the day. We trust they will spare no pains to furnish us with drawings of events as they may occur. We would also remind them that it is necessary to send all sketches, if possible, by the earliest conveyance.

VISIT TO DRED SCOTT—HIS FAMILY—INCIDENTS OF HIS LIFE—DECISION OF THE SUPREME COURT.

WHILE standing in the Fair grounds at St. Louis, and engaged in conversation with a prominent citizen of that enterprising city, he suddenly asked us if we would not like to be introduced to Dred Scott. Upon expressing a desire to be thus honored, the gentleman called to an old negro who was standing near by, and our wish was gratified. Dred made a rude obeisance to our recognition, and seemed to enjoy the notice we expended upon him. We found him on examination to be a pure-blooded African, perhaps fifty years of age, with a shrewd, intelligent, good-natured face, of rather light frame, being not more than five feet six inches high. After some general remarks we expressed a wish to get his portrait (we had made

ELIZA AND LIZZIE, CHILDREN OF DRED SCOTT.

efforts before, through correspondents, and failed), and asked him if he would not go to Fitzgibbon's gallery and

have it taken. The gentleman present explained to Dred that it was proper he should have his likeness in the "great illustrated paper of the country," overruled his many objections, which seemed to grow out of a superstitious feeling, and he promised to be at the gallery the next day. This appointment Dred did not keep. Determined not to be foiled, we sought an interview with Mr. Crane, Dred's lawyer, who promptly gave us a letter of introduction, explaining to Dred that it was to his advantage to have his picture taken to be engraved for our paper, and also directions where we could find his domicile. We found the place with difficulty, the streets in Dred's neighborhood being more clearly defined in the plan of the city than on the mother earth; we finally reached a wooden house, however, protected by a balcony that answered the description. Approaching the door, we saw a smart, tidy-looking negress, perhaps thirty years of age, who, with two female assistants, was busy ironing. To our question, "Is this where Dred Scott lives?" we received, rather hesitatingly, the answer, "Yes." Upon our asking if he was home, she said,

"What white man arter dad nigger for?—why don't white man 'tend to his own business, and let dat nigger 'lone? Some of dese days dey'll steal dat nigger—dat are a fact."

DRED SCOTT. PHOTOGRAPHED BY FITZGIBBON, OF ST. LOUIS.   HIS WIFE, HARRIET. PHOTOGRAPHED BY FITZGIBBON, OF ST. LOUIS.

of this time. The court finally scheduled the retrial for February 2, 1849. But the court's schedule was too full. The retrial was pushed back to May.

In the spring of 1849, a cholera epidemic swept through Saint Louis. More than 4,000 people died from the disease. Hundreds of people fled the city. But Harriet and Dred had to stay within the city limits. They were under the sheriff's supervision. They were hired out to work for two doctors. Dred may have helped treat patients and bury dead people. Harriet may have washed disease-infected bedding and clothing. Harriet and Dred were exposed to cholera, but neither came down with the disease.

Not many people were willing to serve on juries in Saint Louis during the cholera epidemic. The court decided to push back its cases until after the outbreak ended. Then on May 17, another disaster struck the city. A steamboat in a harbor caught on fire. The fire spread

Journalists wrote about the Scotts as their cases became well known throughout the United States.

SUING FOR FREEDOM

Before the Scotts' cases, other enslaved people had sued their slaveholders. Sisters Marguerite, Celeste, and Catiche Scypion sued their slaveholders in 1805. A law made it illegal to enslave Native Americans. The sisters argued that because they were part Native American, they could not be legally enslaved. They won their freedom. In other cases, slaveholders kidnapped and enslaved free black people. Some of these people successfully sued for their freedom. Manisha Sinha is a professor of American history at the University of Connecticut. She says, "We normally don't think of slaves as a part of the abolition movement. But they very much were."

to buildings along the shore. It destroyed hundreds of buildings. The cholera epidemic continued while people tried to rebuild the city. The epidemic did not end until the fall.

In December 1849, Adeline agreed to talk to the Scotts' lawyers. She confirmed that the Scotts were under Emerson's control. Her statement was used as evidence in the Scotts' retrial. On January 12, 1850, the Scotts' cases were finally heard again. This time, the

THE ENSLAVED POPULATION

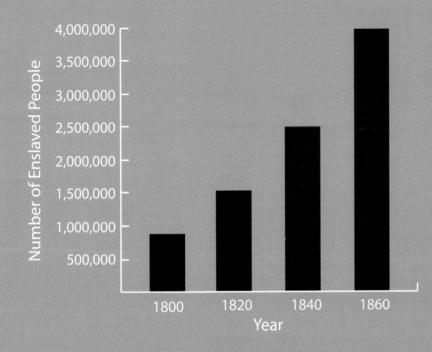

The above graph shows the number of enslaved people in the United States in the years leading up to the American Civil War (1861–1865). What can you tell about slavery in the United States by looking at this graph? How did the enslaved population change throughout the 1800s?

jury ruled in the Scotts' favor. The Scotts were declared free. But their freedom would not last long.

BACK TO COURT

Emerson was not happy with the jury's ruling. Emerson and her brother, John Sanford, appealed to the Missouri

In 2007 an exhibit was created to honor the Scotts at the Old Courthouse in Saint Louis, Missouri.

Supreme Court. Before the Scotts' cases came to trial again, the two cases were combined into one. The case was called *Dred Scott v. Irene Emerson.*

Two more years passed before the case went to trial. By this time, Emerson had handed the case over to her brother. In March 1852, the Missouri Supreme Court heard the case. The court reversed the earlier ruling. It declared that the Scotts were not free.

PRESSING ON

The Scotts did not give up. They filed a lawsuit against Sanford in a federal court. Lawyer Roswell Field took their case for free.

In May 1854, the circuit court ruled in favor of Sanford. But Field was not discouraged. He wanted to take the Scotts' case to the US Supreme Court. The Supreme Court is the most powerful court in the United States. It could overturn the lower court's ruling.

FURTHER EVIDENCE

Chapter Three covers some of the courtroom trials the Scotts went through in their fight for freedom. Identify one of the chapter's main points. What evidence does the author provide to support this point? Read the article at the website below. Does the information on the website support this point? Does it present new evidence?

THE SCOTTS' FIGHT FOR FREEDOM
abdocorelibrary.com/harriet-robinson-scott

CHAPTER
FOUR

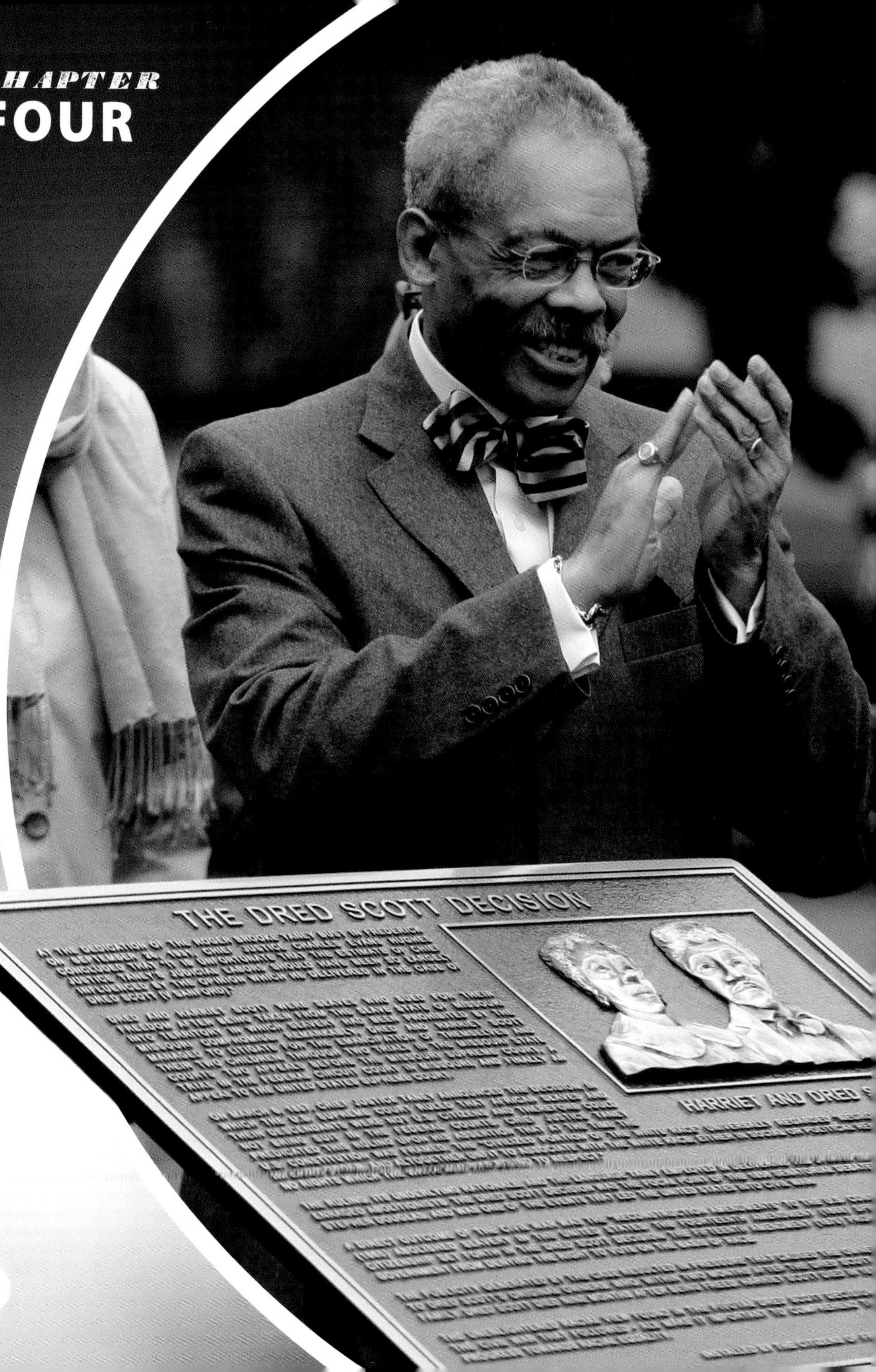

THE FINAL DECISION

Roswell Field appealed to the US Supreme Court in December 1854. The court decided to hear the Scotts' case. The case was called *Dred Scott v. Sanford*. Even though only Dred was named, the decision would also apply to Harriet and their children.

Field arranged for Montgomery Blair to represent Dred. Blair was a famous lawyer. He was not an abolitionist, but he opposed the expansion of slavery. The Scotts' lawsuit was becoming well known throughout the country. People on both sides of the slavery debate were following the case.

A plaque honoring Dred and Harriet Scott was unveiled in Frederick, Maryland, in 2009.

The trial began in February 1856. Blair presented his argument to the Supreme Court justices. He said that when enslaved people moved to a free state, they were free. If they moved back to a slave state, they could not be enslaved again. He also claimed that an African American could be a citizen of the United States. At the time, even free African Americans were not considered citizens. They did not have the same rights as white people.

The Supreme Court delivered its decision on March 6, 1857. Many of the justices were proslavery. Seven of the nine justices said that the Scotts were slaves. Chief Justice Roger B. Taney stated that African Americans were not US citizens. Only citizens can bring a lawsuit to a federal court. Therefore, he said that the Scotts had no right to sue.

The Supreme Court's decision was final. There was no other court for the Scotts to appeal to. They remained enslaved.

MORE CONFLICT

The Supreme Court's decision caused the tension over slavery to reach a crisis point. Presidential candidate Abraham Lincoln disagreed with the *Dred Scott v. Sanford* decision. Lincoln was part of a new political party called the Republican Party. Many northern abolitionists were Republicans. They supported the Scotts' right to freedom.

The Democratic Party opposed the Republican Party. Many southern slaveholders were Democrats. They agreed with the *Dred Scott v. Sanford* decision.

PERSPECTIVES
EQUALITY FOR SOME

Roger B. Taney was the chief justice of the Supreme Court when the Scotts' case was heard. Taney believed African Americans were inferior to white people. He used the Declaration of Independence to defend his belief. The Declaration of Independence states that all men are created equal. But because white people had written the document, Taney believed that it did not apply to African Americans.

Abraham Lincoln was president of the United States from 1861 to 1865.

In 1860 Lincoln won the presidential election. The conflict between the northern and southern states escalated. Eleven southern states left the Union. They formed the Confederate States of America, or the Confederacy. The northern states made up the Union. In 1861 war broke out between the Union and the Confederacy. This conflict was the American Civil War (1861–1865).

FREE AT LAST

The Civil War ended in 1865. The Union won the war, and the southern states rejoined the country. Then the US Congress passed the Thirteenth Amendment. This amendment freed all enslaved people in the United States. But the Scotts did not have to wait that long. In about 1850, Emerson remarried. Her new husband was Calvin Chaffee. Chaffee was a Massachusetts congressman and an abolitionist. When he married Emerson, he had not known that she was a slaveholder. He made this discovery during the Dred Scott v. Sanford trial. As soon as the trial ended, Chaffee

AN UNWELCOME SURPRISE

Congressman Calvin Chaffee found out Emerson owned the Scotts shortly before the Supreme Court gave its decision in Dred Scott v. Sanford. Newspapers around the country criticized him for being an abolitionist who owned slaves. Because of the negative publicity, Chaffee did not run for reelection in 1858.

transferred ownership of the Scott family to Dred's friend, Henry Blow. On May 26, 1857, Blow granted the Scotts their freedom.

Dred was not able to enjoy his freedom for long. In 1858 he died from the disease tuberculosis. Harriet remained in Saint Louis with her children. She worked as a laundress for many years. She washed and cleaned people's clothes. She died on June 17, 1876, at the age of 61.

It had been illegal for enslaved people to read or write. Because of this, Harriet had never learned these skills. She was not able to record her experiences. The public only knew her as Dred's wife. But she had accomplished something extraordinary. Harriet and Dred's decision to sue for their family's freedom took courage and determination. Harriet had just wanted her children to be free. But her actions pushed the nation in a direction that would eventually bring an end to slavery in the United States.

STRAIGHT TO THE
SOURCE

African American abolitionist Frederick Douglass made a speech after the *Dred Scott v. Sanford* decision was announced. Douglass had escaped slavery and spoke out against it. His speech was given to the American Anti-Slavery Society in New York. He said:

> The Supreme Court of the United States is not the only power in this world. It is very great, but the Supreme Court of the Almighty is greater. Judge Taney can do many things, but he cannot perform impossibilities. He cannot bale out the ocean, annihilate the firm old earth, or pluck the silvery star of liberty from our Northern sky. He may decide, and decide again; but he cannot reverse the decision of the Most High. He cannot change the essential nature of things—making evil good, and good evil.

Source: "Frederick Douglass Project Writings: The Dred Scott Decision." *The University of Rochester*. The University of Rochester, n.d. Web. Accessed October 23, 2018.

Consider Your Audience

Adapt this passage for a different audience, such as your friends. Write a blog post conveying this same information for the new audience. How does your post differ from the original text and why?

FAST FACTS

- Harriet Robinson was born into slavery in Virginia in about 1820.

- When she was about 14 years old, Harriet moved to Fort Snelling on the frontier with her slaveholder. Fort Snelling was in a free territory.

- At Fort Snelling, Harriet met and married another enslaved person named Dred Scott. Harriet and Dred Scott lived for a while at Fort Snelling.

- The Scotts had two daughters. The Scotts wanted their children to be free. They decided to sue in the courts for their freedom. They had lived for a time in free territories, so they argued that they should be free.

- The Scotts' case went to the Supreme Court in 1857. The Supreme Court decided that the Scotts were property, not citizens. Since they were not citizens, they could not file lawsuits. This decision led to more disagreements among Americans about slavery. These disagreements led to the American Civil War.

- The Scott family gained their freedom after the Supreme Court case in 1857. Dred died in 1858. Harriet later died in 1876.

STOP AND
THINK

Tell the Tale

Chapter One of this book describes Harriet's first years at Fort Snelling. Imagine you lived in the fort at that time. Write a journal entry about your experiences.

Surprise Me

Chapter Three discusses the Scotts' long battle in courts for their freedom. After reading this book, what two or three facts about their trials did you find most surprising? Write a few sentences about each fact. Why did you find each fact surprising?

You Are There

Chapter Four discusses the *Dred Scott v. Sanford* Supreme Court trial. Imagine you are in the courtroom during the trial. Write a letter home telling your family or friends about the experience. Be sure to add plenty of detail to your letter.

GLOSSARY

abolish
to officially end or do away with something

abolitionist
someone who was against slavery

amendment
a change or an addition to an existing law

appeal
an attempt to overturn a court's ruling by retrying a case in a higher court, such as the US Supreme Court

compromise
an agreement in which each side involved gives up something in order to end an argument

epidemic
an outbreak of a disease that affects many people within a particular region

jury
a group of people at a trial that decides whether a person accused of a crime is guilty or not

lawsuit
a case that is brought against a person or group in a court

petition
a formal request asking to have a legal case decided by a court

sue
to file a lawsuit

ONLINE
RESOURCES

To learn more about Harriet Robinson Scott, visit our free resource websites below.

Visit **abdocorelibrary.com** or scan this QR code for free Common Core resources for teachers and students, including vetted activities, multimedia, and booklinks, for deeper subject comprehension.

Visit **abdobooklinks.com** or scan this QR code for free additional online weblinks for further learning. These links are routinely monitored and updated to provide the most current information available.

LEARN
MORE

Halls, Kelly Milner. *Life during the Civil War*. Minneapolis, MN: Abdo Publishing, 2015.

Rissman, Rebecca. *Slavery in the United States*. Minneapolis, MN: Abdo Publishing, 2015.

ABOUT THE
AUTHORS

Duchess Harris, JD, PhD

Dr. Harris is a professor of American Studies at Macalester College and curator of the Duchess Harris Collection of ABDO books. She is also the coauthor of the titles in the collection, which features popular selections such as *Hidden Human Computers: The Black Women of NASA* and series including News Literacy and Being Female in America.

Before working with ABDO, Dr. Harris authored several other books on the topics of race, culture, and American history. She served as an associate editor for *Litigation News*, the American Bar Association Section of Litigation's quarterly flagship publication, and was the first editor in chief of *Law Raza*, an interactive online journal covering race and the law, published at William Mitchell College of Law. She has earned a PhD in American Studies from the University of Minnesota and a JD from William Mitchell College of Law.

Samantha S. Bell

Samantha S. Bell lives with her family in upstate South Carolina. She graduated from Furman University with a degree in history and a teaching certification in social studies. She is the author of more than 90 nonfiction books for children.

INDEX